# 40 Ahadith Series

## Lofty Status of Parents

**THE WORLD FEDERATION**
OF KHOJA SHIA ITHNA-ASHERI MUSLIM COMMUNITIES
www.world-federation.org

British Library Cataloguing-in-Publication Data
A catalogue record for this book is available from the British Library

ISBN 1-898449-87-8

© Copyright 2005 the World Federation of KSIMC

**Published by**
The Islamic Education Board of the
World Federation of Khoja Shia Ithna-Asheri Muslim Communities
Registered Charity in the UK No. 282 0
Islamic Centre - Wood Lane
Stanmore, Middlesex
United Kingdom
HA7 4LQ
www.world-federation.org/ieb
ieb@world-federation.org

**North America Sales and Distribution**
Islāmic Humanitarian Service · 81 Hollinger Crescent · Kitchener, Ontario
Canada, N2K 2Y8 · Tel: 519-576-7111 · Fax: 519-576-8378
**ihs@primus.ca · www.al-haqq.com**

**Africa Sales & Distribution**
Tabligh Sub Committtee - K.S.I. Jamā'at – Dar Es Salaam · P.O. Box 2
Dar es Salaam, Tanzania · Tel: 255-22-211-5119 Fax: 255-22-211- 107
**tabligh@raha.com · www.dartabligh.org**

In the Name of Allāh, the Most Gracious, the Most Merciful

## Introduction

The Noble Prophet (peace be upon him and his family) has said:

مَنْ حَفِظَ عَلَى أُمَّتِي أَرْبَعِينَ حَدِيثًا يَنْتَفِعُونَ بِهَا بَعَثَهُ اللَّهُ يَوْمَ الْقِيَامَةِ فَقِيهاً عَالِماً.

*"The person from amongst my nation who memorizes forty traditions pertaining to those issues of religion which he is in need of, Allāh shall resurrect him on the Day of Judgment as a scholar with a deep insight into the faith."*

In following the above ḥadīth, The Islamic Education Board of The World Federation of KSIMC (IEB - WF) has decided to publish a series of booklets of 40 aḥādīth on different subjects. The aḥādīth, which have been selected from various sources, are short and simple and therefore easy to understand and memorize. It is envisaged that the booklets will not only be useful for Zakireen, Madrasah teachers and students, but will be of benefit to the Ummah at large.

The collection of the aḥādīth, together with their translation in English, was carried out by Shaykh Shahnawaz Mahdavi. IEB - WF would like to thank the Shaykh Mahdavi for his efforts in the compilation and translation of this work. May Allāh (Glory and Greatness be to Him) accept this work as a further attempt by IEB - WF to propagate Islām.

# TABLE OF CONTENTS

| | |
|---|---|
| Introduction | 11 |
| The Greatest Obligatory Act | 15 |
| The Best of Deeds | 16 |
| Attachment to Parents | 17 |
| The Most Beloved Deed | 18 |
| Looking at Parents | 19 |
| The Great Rank of Parents | 20 |
| Kindness to Parents | 21 |
| Obedience Towards One's Parents | 22 |
| The Most Exalted Station | 23 |
| Repayment Of Debts | 24 |
| Pleasing Parents | 25 |
| Sheltered by the 'Arsh [Throne] of Allāh | 26 |
| Travel and be Good! | 27 |
| Increase in Life and Livelihood | 28 |

| | |
|---|---|
| Benefits of Kindness to Parents | 29 |
| First and Foremost - be Good to your Mother | 30 |
| You Shall Reap What You Sow! | 31 |
| The Rights of the Father | 32 |
| Worship In Looking | 33 |
| Meaning of Good Conduct | 34 |
| Responsibilities Towards One's Parents | 35 |
| On Behalf of Parents | 36 |
| Evil Parents And Kindness | 37 |
| Polytheist Parents | 38 |
| Visiting The Graves Of Parents | 39 |
| Kindness To Parents And Paradise | 40 |
| A Stern Look | 41 |
| A Hateful Look | 42 |
| Making the Parents Sad | 43 |
| The Imam's Displeasure | 44 |

| | |
|---|---:|
| Quarrelling with One's Father | 45 |
| Fragrance Of Paradise | 46 |
| No Entry Into Paradise! | 47 |
| Allāh Shall Not Exhibit Mercy Upon Them! | 48 |
| Chastisement In This World | 49 |
| The Grave Sin | 50 |
| Wretchedness | 51 |
| Perdition | 52 |
| Acts Without Benefits | 54 |
| Forgiveness Of Sins | 55 |

## Introduction

Although our existence is from Allāh (Glory and Greatness be to Him), it is our parents who are the means of giving us life. We are an offshoot of their existence and a fruit of the garden of their unparalleled affection, training, love and sentiments.

When the forgetful human being grows up to become big and strong and comes to acquire a certain credibility (in life), he forgets the period wherein he was weak and lacking in strength. He disregards the exhaustive efforts of his parents; what ingratitude could be worse than this?

Humanity and ethics demand that we safeguard these two jewels (our mother and father) - by exhibiting goodness towards them while they are alive, and by means of charity and goodly remembrance after their death.

Our lives are an extension of our parent's lives while our children's lives are a continuation of ours. Our good behavior towards our parents and our exhibition of kindness towards them shall cause our children to grow up as grateful and righteous individuals. They shall behave with us just as we have behaved with our own parents.

Just as it is beyond our means to fulfill the rights of Allāh (Glory and Greatness be to Him) and to thank Him for all His bounties in their entirety, similarly we can never thank our parents sufficiently for their efforts. The only thing that we can do is to acknowledge our inability and submit ourselves, in humility and reverence, before these two angels. However, comprehension of their status in the eyes of Allāh (Glory and Greatness be to Him) paves the way to fulfill some of their numerous rights.

The traditions that we shall read in this collection of forty traditions shall serve to make us aware of some of our responsibilities towards our parents.

May Allāh (Glory and Greatness be to Him) grant us the Divine success that we may come be regarded amongst those who have been good towards their parents.

"O' Allāh! Make us such that we may be grateful for the efforts of our parents."

"O' Allāh! Make us successful in bringing forth a generation of pure-hearted, believing, grateful and righteous individuals."

﴿ وَ قَضَىٰ رَبُّكَ أَلاَّ تَعْبُدُوا إِلاَّ إِيَّاهُ وَ بِالْوَالدَيْنِ إِحْسَاناً إِمَّا يَبْلُغَنَّ عِنْدَكَ الْكِبَرَ أَحَدُهُمَا أَوْ كِلاَهُمَا فَلاَ تَقُلْ لَهُمَا أُفٍّ وَ لاَ تَنْهَرْهُمَا وَ قُلْ لَهُمَا قَوْلاً كَرِيــماً ﴾

*"And your Lord has commanded that you shall not serve (any) but Him, and that you shall show goodness to your parents. If either or both of them reach old age with you, say not to them (so much as) "Ugh" nor chide them, and speak to them a generous word."*

Noble Qur'an, Sūrat Banī Isrā'īl (17) Verse 23

## Ḥadīth Number 1
## The Greatest Obligatory Act

عَنْ أَمِيرِ الْمُؤْمِنِينَ عليه السلام أَنَّهُ قَالَ: بِرُّ الْوَالِدَيْنِ أَكْبَرُ فَرِيضَةٍ.

The Commander of the Faithful (peace be upon him) has said: "Goodness towards (one's) parents is the greatest obligatory act."

Mizānul Ḥikmah, Volume 10, Page 709

## Ḥadīth Number 2
## The Best of Deeds

قَالَ الصَّادِقُ عليه السلام: أَفْضَلُ الأَعْمَالِ الصَّلَاةُ لِوَقْتِهَا وَ بِرُّ الْوَالِدَينِ وَ الْجِهَادُ فِي سَبِيلِ اللّهِ.

Imām as-Ṣādiq (peace be upon him) has said: "The best deeds are: Ṣalāt in its stipulated hour, goodness towards parents and Jihād in the way of Allāh."

Biḥārul Anwār, Volume 74, Page 85

## Ḥadīth Number 3
## Attachment to Parents

فَقَالَ رَسُولُ اللّٰهِ ﷺ: فَقِرَّ مَعَ وَالِدَيْكَ فَوَ الَّذِي نَفْسِي بِيَدِهِ لَأُنْسُهُمَا بِكَ يَوْماً وَ لَيْلَةً خَيْرٌ مِنْ جِهَادِ سَنَةٍ.

[A person once approached the Messenger of Allāh (peace be upon him and his family) and said: "I have an old father and mother, who due to their attachment towards me, are not keen for me to go to Jihād."]

[Hearing this], the Noble Prophet (peace be upon him and his family) said: "(If such is the case then) Stay with your parents for by the One in whose control lies my soul! Their attachment of one day and one night to you is better than one year of Jihād."

Biḥārul Anwār, Volume 74, Page 82

## Ḥadīth Number 4
## The Most Beloved Deed

سَأَلْتُ رَسُولَ اللهِ ﷺ: أَيُّ الأَعْمَالِ أَحَبُّ إِلَـــى اللهِ عَزَّ وَ جَلَّ؟ قَالَ الصَّلَاةُ لِوَقْتِهَا. قُلْتُ ثُمَّ أَيُّ شَيْءٍ؟ قَالَ بِرُّ الْوَالِدَينِ. قُلْتُ ثُمَّ أَيُّ شَيْءٍ؟ قَالَ الْجِهَادُ فِي سَبِيلِ اللهِ.

[Ibne ʿAbbās states:] "I questioned the Messenger of Allāh (peace be upon him and his family): Which deed is the most beloved in the eyes of Allāh, the Mighty, the Glorious?" He (peace be upon him and his family) replied: "(Offering) prayers at their stipulated times." I then asked: "Which is the next most beloved deed?" He (peace be upon him and his family) answered: "Goodness towards (one's) parents." I asked him again: "After this which is the most beloved act?" He (peace be upon him and his family) said: "Jihād in the way of Allāh."

Biḥārul Anwār, Volume 74, Page 70

## Ḥadīth Number 5
## Looking at Parents

قَالَ رَسُولُ اللَّهِ ﷺ: مَا مِنْ وَلَدٍ بَارٍّ نَظَرَ إِلَـى أَبَوَيْهِ بِرَحْمَةٍ إِلَّا كَانَ لَهُ بِكُلِّ نَظْرَةٍ حَجَّةٌ مَبْرُورَةٌ. فَقَالُوا يَا رَسُولَ اللَّهِ وَ إِنْ نَظَرَ فِي كُلِّ يَوْمٍ مِائَةَ نَظْرَةٍ؟ قَالَ نَعَمْ. أَللَّهُ أَكْبَرُ وَ أَطْيَبُ.

The Messenger of Allāh (peace be upon him and his family) said: "Every righteous child who casts a look of mercy and affection upon his parents shall be granted, for every look of his, rewards equivalent to that of an accepted Ḥajj." Those around the Prophet questioned: "O' Prophet of Allāh! Even if he were to look at them a hundred times a day?" The Messenger of Allāh (peace be upon him and his family) replied: "Indeed! Allāh is the Greatest and Most Kind."

Biḥārul Anwār, Volume 74, Page 73

## Ḥadīth Number 6
## The Great Rank of Parents

عَنْ أَبِي الْحَسَنِ الرِّضَا ﷺ قَالَ: إِنَّ اللَّهَ أَمَرَ بِثَلاَثَةٍ مَقْرُونٍ بِهَا ثَلاَثَةٌ أُخْرَى: أَمَرَ بِالصَّلاَةِ وَ الزَّكَاةِ فَمَنْ صَلَّى وَ لَمْ يُزَكِّ لَمْ تُقْبَلْ مِنْهُ صَلاَتُهُ وَ أَمَرَ بِالشُّكْرِ لَهُ وَ لِلْوَالِدَيْنِ فَمَنْ لَمْ يَشْكُرْ وَالِدَيْهِ لَمْ يَشْكُرِ اللَّهَ وَ أَمَرَ بِاتِّقَاءِ اللَّهِ وَ صِلَةِ الرَّحِمِ فَمَنْ لَمْ يَصِلْ رَحِمَهُ لَمْ يَتَّقِ اللَّهَ.

Imām al-Ridhā (peace be upon him) has said: "Allāh, the Mighty, the Glorious, has commanded three things with which he has associated three other things. He associated payment of zakāt along with prayers such that one who offers prayers, but desists from offering zakāt, his prayers are rejected. He associated gratitude to Him with gratitude towards parents such that one who is grateful to Allāh, but ungrateful to his parents, will be deemed as ungrateful to Allāh. He associated righteousness with bonds of kinship such that one who is righteous, but has severed relations with his kin, will be deemed as not being righteous."

Biḥārul Anwār, Volume 74, Page 77

## Ḥadīth Number 7
## Kindness to Parents

قَالَ الصَّادِقُ ﷷ: بِرُّ الْوَالِدَيْنِ مِنْ حُسْنِ مَعْرِفَةِ الْعَبْدِ بِاللّٰهِ إِذْ لاَ عِبَادَةَ أَسْرَعُ بُلُوغاً بِصَاحِبِهَا إِلَى رِضَى اللّٰهِ مِنْ بِرِّ الْوَالِدَيْنِ الْمُسْلِمَيْنِ لِوَجْهِ اللّٰهِ.

Imām as-Ṣādiq (peace be upon him) has said: "Goodness towards the parents is an indication of a person's excellent cognizance of Allāh. This is because there is no worship that can take a person towards the happiness of Allāh faster than exhibiting respect towards his Muslim parents for the sake of Allāh."

Biḥārul Anwār, Volume 74, pg.77

## Ḥadīth Number 8
## Obedience Towards One's Parents

قَالَ رَسُولُ اللّٰهِ ﷺ: مَنْ أَصْبَحَ مُطِيعاً لِلّٰهِ فِي الْوَالَدَينِ أَصْبَحَ لَهُ بَابَانِ مَفْتُوحَانِ مِنَ الْجَنَّةِ وَ إِنْ كَانَ وَاحِداً فَوَاحِداً.

The Messenger of Allāh (peace be upon him and his family) said: "One, who follows the orders of Allāh with regards to obeying parents, shall have two doors of Paradise opened up for him. And if there happens to be only one parent, one door of Paradise shall open up for him."

Kanzul 'Ummāl, Volume 16, Page 67

## Ḥadīth Number 9
## The Most Exalted Station

قَالَ رَسُولُ اللّٰهِ ﷺ: أَلْعَبْدُ الْمُطِيعُ لِوَالِدَيْهِ وَ لِرَبِّهِ فِي أَعْلَىٰ عِلِّيِّينَ.

The Messenger of Allāh (peace be upon him and his family) has stated: "One who is obedient towards his parents and his Lord shall be accommodated in the most exalted of places on the Day of Judgment."

Kanzul 'Ummāl, Volume 16, Page 467

## Hadīth Number 10
## Repayment Of Debts

عَنْ رَسُولِ اللّٰهِ ﷺ: مَنْ حَجَّ عَنْ وَالِدَيهِ أَوْ قَضىٰ عَنْهُمَا مَغْرَماً بَعَثَهُ اللّٰهُ يَوْمَ الْقِيَامَةِ مَعَ الْأَبْرَارِ.

The Messenger of Allāh (peace be upon him and his family) has said: "One who performs Ḥajj on behalf of his parents and repays their debts shall be raised by Allah on the Day of Judgement amongst the righteous ones."

Kanzul 'Ummāl, Volume 16, Page 468

## Ḥadīth Number 11
## Pleasing Parents

قَالَ رَسُولُ اللّٰهِ ﷺ: مَنْ أَرْضَىٰ وَالِدَيْهِ فَقَدْ أَرْضَىٰ اللّٰهَ وَ مَنْ أَسْخَطَ وَالِدَيْهِ فَقَدَ أَسْخَطَ اللّٰهَ.

The Messenger of Allāh (peace be upon him and his family) said: "One who pleases his parents has verily pleased Allāh, and one who has angered his parents has verily angered Allāh."

Kanzul 'Ummāl, Volume 16, Page 470

## Ḥadīth Number 12
## Sheltered by the 'Arsh [Throne] of Allāh

عَنِ الصَّادِقِ ﷺ: قَالَ بَيْنَا مُوسىٰ بْنِ عِمْرَانَ يُنَاجِي رَبَّهُ عَزَّ وَ جَلَّ إِذْ رَأَى رَجُلاً تَحْتَ ظِلِّ عَرْشِ اللّٰهِ عَزَّ وَ جَلَّ. فَقَالَ: يَا رَبِّ مَنْ هٰذَا الَّذِي قَدْ أَظَلَّهُ عَرْشُكَ؟ فَقَالَ: هٰذَا كَانَ بَارًّا بِوَالِدَيْهِ وَ لَمْ يَمْشِ بِالنَّمِيمَةِ.

Imām as-Ṣādiq (peace be upon him) related: "Once when Prophet Mūsā (peace be upon him) was engaged in a conversation with his Lord, The Mighty, The Glorious, he observed a person beneath the 'Arsh (Throne) of Allāh, whereupon he (peace be upon him) asked: O' My Lord! Who is this person, who is being sheltered by Your 'Arsh?" Allāh replied: "This person had been kind and good towards his parents and never indulged in slandering (them)."

Biḥārul Anwār, Volume 74, Page 65

## Hadīth Number 13
## Travel and be Good!

قَالَ رَسُولُ اللّهِ ﷺ: سِرْ سَنَتَيْنِ بَرَّ وَالِدَيْكَ سِرْ سَنَةً صِلْ رَحِمَكَ.

The Messenger of Allāh (peace be upon him and his family) said: "Travel even for two years to do good to your parents. Journey (even) for one year to establish bonds of kinship (with your relatives)."

Biḥārul Anwār, Volume 74, Page 83

## Ḥadīth Number 14
## Increase in Life and Livelihood

قَالَ رَسُولُ اللَّهِ ﷺ: مَنْ أَحَبَّ أَنْ يَمُدَّ لَهُ عُمْرَهُ وَ أَنْ يَزْدَادُ فِي رِزْقِهِ فَلْـيَبِرْ وَالِدَيْهِ وَ لْـيَصِلْ رَحِمَهُ.

The Messenger of Allāh (peace be upon him and his family) said: "One who desires a long life and an increase in livelihood should exhibit goodness towards his parents and establish bonds of kinship (with his relatives)."

Kanzul 'Ummāl, Volume 16, Page 475

## Ḥadīth Number 15
## Benefits of Kindness to Parents

فَقَالَ أَبُو عَبْدِ اللّٰهِ ﷺ: يَا مُيَسِّرُ قَدْ حَضَرَ أَجْلُكَ غَيْرُ مَرَّةٍ وَ لاَ مَرَّتَيْنِ كُلُّ ذٰلِكَ يُؤَخِّرُ اللّٰهُ أَجَلَكَ لِصِلَّتِكَ قُرَابَتِكَ وَ إِنْ كُنْتَ تُرِيدُ أَنْ يُزَادَ فِي عُمْرِكَ فَبِرْ شَيْخَيْكَ يَعْنِي أَبَوَيْهِ.

[Hanān Ibn Sudaïr narrates: "We were in the presence of Imām aṣ-Ṣādiq (peace be upon him) and amidst us was Muyassir. During the discussion, the topic of ṣilah raḥim (establishing bonds of kinship with one's relatives) came to the fore, whereupon] the Imām (peace be upon him), [addressing Muyassir], said: 'O' Muyassir! On several occasions, your end had drawn near, but on each occasion, Allāh delayed your death due to your acts of ṣilah raḥim with your relatives. If you desire to have your life-span increased, exhibit goodness and kindness towards your parents.'"

Biḥārul Anwār, Volume 74, Page 84

## Ḥadīth Number 16
## First and Foremost - be Good to your Mother

عَنْ أَبِي عَبْدِ اللهِ ﷺ: قَالَ جَاءَ رَجُلٌ إِلَى النَّبِيِّ ﷺ فَقَالَ: يَا رَسُولَ اللهِ مَنْ أَبَرُّ؟ قَالَ أُمَّكَ. قَالَ ثُمَّ مَنْ؟ قَالَ أُمَّكَ. قَالَ ثُمَّ مَنْ؟ قَالَ أُمَّكَ. قَالَ ثُمَّ مَنْ؟ قَالَ أَبَاكَ.

Imām as-Ṣādiq (peace be upon him) relates that once a person approached the Noble Prophet (peace be upon him and his family) and asked: "O' Prophet of Allāh! Towards whom should I exhibit goodness and kindness?" The Noble Prophet replied: "Towards your mother." The man then asked: "And after that towards whom?" The Noble Prophet again said: "Your Mother." He asked again: "And then?" Once again, he replied: "Your mother." For the fourth time the man asked: "And then?" This time he said: "(Then towards) Your father."

Biḥārul Anwār, Volume 74, Page 49

## Ḥadīth Number 17
## As You Sow so Shall You Reap!

عَنْ رَسُولِ اللهِ ﷺ: بِرُّوا آبَاءَكُمْ يَـبِرُّكُمْ أَبْنَاءُكُمْ. عِفُّوا عَنْ نِسَاءِ النَّاسِ تُعَفُّ نِسَاءُكُمْ.

The Messenger of Allāh (peace be upon him and his family) has said: "Be good towards your parents and your children will be good towards you. (And) Look upon the womenfolk of others with purity (in conduct and intention) and your womenfolk will be looked upon with purity."

Kanzul 'Ummāl, Volume 16, Page 466

## Ḥadīth Number 18
## The Rights of the Father

عَنْ أَبِي الْحَسَنِ عَلِيِّ بنِ مُوسَى عليه السلام قَالَ: سَأَلَ رَجُلٌ رَسُولَ اللّه صلى الله عليه وآله مَا حَقُّ الْوَالِدِ عَلَى وَلَدِهِ؟ قَالَ: لاَ يُسَمِّيهِ بِاسْمِهِ وَ لاَ يَمْشِي بَيْنَ يَدَيْهِ وَ لاَ يَجْلِسُ قَبْلَهُ وَ لاَ يَسْتَسِبُّ لَهُ.

Imām ar-Riḍā (peace be upon him) narrates that a person once asked the Messenger of Allāh (peace be upon him and his family): "What are the rights of the father upon the son?" The Noble Prophet replied: "He should not call his father by name, he should not walk ahead of him, he should not sit until his father has seated himself and he should not do such acts as a result of which people abuse his father."

Biḥārul Anwār, Volume 74, Page 45

## Ḥadīth Number 19
## Worship In Looking

قَالَ رَسُولُ اللّٰهِ ﷺ: نَظَرُ الْوَلَدِ إِلَىٰ وَالِدَيْهِ حُبًّا لَهُمَا عِبَادَةٌ.

The Messenger of Allāh (peace be upon him and his family) has said: "The look of a child towards his parents out of love for them is an act of worship."

Biḥārul Anwār, Volume 74, Page 80

## Ḥadīth Number 20
## Meaning of Good Conduct

عَنْ أَبِي وَلَّادِ الْحَنَّاطِ قَالَ: سَأَلْتُ أَبَا عَبْدِ اللّٰهِ ﷺ عَنْ قَوْلِ اللّٰهِ عَزَّ وَ جَلَّ ﴿ وَ بِالْوَالِدَيْنِ إِحْسَاناً ﴾ مَا هٰذَا الْإِحْسَانُ؟ فَقَالَ: الْإِحْسَانُ أَنْ تُحْسِنَ صُحْبَتَهُمَا وَ أَنْ لَا تُكَلِّفَهُمَا أَنْ يَسْأَلَاكَ شَيْئاً مِمَّا يَحْتَاجَانِ إِلَيْهِ.

Abu Wallād al-Ḥannāṭ narrates that he once asked Imām as-Ṣādiq (peace be upon him) about the meaning of the words of Allāh (in the Qur'ān): ❮And be good to parents."❯[1]

The Imām (peace be upon him) replied: "Being good to them means to accompany them in a good manner and never to wait for them to ask you for what they need."

Biḥārul Anwār, Volume 74, Page 79

---

[1] Al-Qur'an, Sūratul Baqarah (2), Verse 83

## Ḥadīth Number 21
## Responsibilities Towards One's Parents

قَالَ الصَّادِقُ ﷺ: لاَ تَمْلاَ عَيْنَيْكَ مِنَ النَّظَرِ إِلَيْهِمَا إِلاَ بِرَحْمَةٍ وَ رِقَّةٍ وَ لاَ تَرْفَعْ صَوْتَكَ فَوْقَ أَصْوَاتِهِمَا وَ لاَ يَدَيْكَ فَوْقَ أَيْدِيهِمَا وَ لاَ تَتَقَدَّمْ قُدَّامَهُمَا.

Imām as-Ṣādiq (peace be upon him) has said (in regards to one's parents): "Do not cast your gaze upon them except with love and compassion; do not raise your voice above theirs; do not raise your hands above theirs; do not walk ahead of them."

Biḥārul Anwār, Volume 74, Page 79

## Ḥadīth Number 22
## On Behalf of Parents

قَالَ الصَّادِقُ ﷺ: مَا يَمْنَعُ الرَّجُلَ مِنْكُمْ أَنْ يَبَرَّ وَالِدَيْهِ حَيَّيْنِ وَ مَيِّتَيْنِ يُصَلِّيَ عَنْهُمَا وَ يَتَصَدَّقَ عَنْهُمَا وَ يَحُجَّ عَنْهُمَا وَ يَصُومَ عَنْهُمَا فَيَكُونَ الَّذِي صَنَعَ لَهُمَا وَ لَهُ مِثْلُ ذٰلِكَ فَيَزِيدَهُ اللّٰهُ عَزَّ وَ جَلَّ بِبِرِّهِ وَ صِلَتِهِ خَيْرَاً كَثِيراً.

Imām as-Ṣādiq (peace be upon him) had said: "What prevents a person from doing good to his parents - whether alive or dead - by offering prayers, giving charity, performing Ḥajj on behalf of them, (knowing that) the rewards of these acts are also granted to him, in addition to his parents. Besides, due to his good deeds and prayers (for them), Allāh, the Mighty and the Glorious, shall grant him abundant good."

Biḥārul Anwār, Volume 74, Page 46

## Ḥadīth Number 23
## Evil Parents And Kindness

عَنْ أَبِي جَعْفَرٍ ﷺ قَالَ: ثَلَاثٌ لَمْ يَجْعَلِ اللهُ عَزَّ وَ جَلَّ لِأَحَدٍ فِيهِنَّ رُخْصَةً أَدَاءُ الْأَمَانَةِ إِلَى الْبَرِّ وَ الْفَاجِرِ وَ الْوَفَاءُ بِالْعَهْدِ لِلْبَرِّ وَ الْفَاجِرِ وَ بِرُّ الْوَالِدَيْنِ بَرَّيْنِ كَانَا أَوْ فَاجِرَيْنِ.

Imām Muḥammad al-Bāqir (peace be upon him) has said: "There are three things which Allāh, the Mighty and the Glorious has not permitted anyone to forsake: returning a trust to its owner, irrespective of whether he is a good person or an evil one; fulfilling one's promises and covenants, irrespective of whether it has been made to a good person or an evil one; being good and kind towards one's parents, irrespective of whether they are good or evil."

Biḥārul Anwār, Volume 74, Page 56

## Hadīth Number 24
## Polytheist Parents

عَنِ الرِّضَا عليه السلام فِي كِتَابِهِ إِلَى الْمَأْمُونِ قَالَ: وَ بِرُّ الْوَالِدَيْنِ وَاجِبٌ وَ إِنْ كَانَا مُشْرِكَيْنِ وَ لاَ طَاعَةَ لَهُمَا فِي مَعْصِيَةِ الْخَالِقِ.

In a letter to Ma'mūn, Imām ar-Riḍā (peace be upon him) wrote: "To do good to one's parents is obligatory, even if they are of the polytheists, however, they should not be obeyed in acts that go against the commands of Allāh."

Biḥārul Anwār, Volume 74, Page 72

## Ḥadīth Number 25
## Visiting The Graves Of Parents

قَالَ رَسُولُ اللّٰهِ ﷺ: مَنْ زَارَ قَبْرَ وَالِدَيْهِ أَوْ أَحَدِهِمَا فِي كُلِّ جُمْعَةٍ مَرَّةً غَفَرَ اللّٰهُ لَهُ وَ كَتَبَ لَهُ بَارًّا.

It has been narrated that the Messenger of Allāh (peace be upon him and his family) said: "Whoever visits the graves of his parents or one of them every Friday, Allāh shall forgive his sins and shall regard him to be of those who had been kind to his parents."

Kanzul 'Ummāl, Volume 16, Page 468

## Hadīth Number 26
## Kindness To Parents And Paradise

عَنْ أَبِي الْحَسَنِ عليه السلام قَالَ: قَالَ رَسُولُ اللّٰهِ ﷺ كُنْ بَارًّا وَ اقْتَصِرْ عَلَى الْجَنَّةِ وَ إِنْ كُنْتَ عَاقًّا فَظًّا فَاقْتَصِرْ عَلَى النَّارِ.

Imām ar-Riḍā (peace be upon him) relates that the Noble Prophet (peace be upon him and his family) has said: "Be good and kind to your parents so that your recompense is paradise, and if you have been disowned by them, your abode shall be the fire (of Hell)."

Al-Kāfī, Volume 2, pg.348

## Ḥadīth Number 27
## A Stern Look

عَنْ أَبِي عَبْدِ اللّٰهِ ﷺ قَالَ: لَوْ عَلِمَ اللّٰهُ شَيْئاً أَدْنَىٰ مِنْ أُفٍّ لَنَهَىٰ عَنْهُ وَ هُوَ مِنْ أَدْنَىٰ الْعُقُوقِ وَ مِنَ الْعُقُوقِ أَنْ يَنْظُرَ الرَّجُلُ إِلَىٰ وَالِدَيْهِ فَيُحِدَّ النَّظَرَ إِلَيْهِمَا.

Imām as-Ṣādiq (peace be upon him) has said: "Had Allāh known of a thing more trivial and insignificant than the word 'ugh', he would have forbidden it (to be spoken to the parents). Uttering 'ugh' (to the parents) is the mildest form of ill conduct towards the parents. One of the ways in which a person can be regarded as being disowned by the parents is that he casts a hard and stern look upon them."

Al-Kāfī, Volume 4, Page 50

## Ḥadīth Number 28
## A Hateful Look

عَنْ أَبِي عَبْدِ اللهِ ﷺ قَالَ: مَنْ نَظَرَ إِلَى أَبَوَيْهِ نَظَرَ مَاقِتٍ وَ هُمَا ظَالِمَانِ لَهُ لَمْ يَقْبَلِ اللَّهُ لَهُ صَلَاةً.

Imām as-Ṣādiq (peace be upon him) has said: "Allāh shall not accept the prayers of a person who looks at his parents with hatred, even if they have been unfair to him!"

Al-Kāfi, Volume 4, Page 50

## Hadīth Number 29
## Making the Parents Sad

قَالَ أَمِيرُ الْمُؤْمِنِينَ ﷺ: مَنْ أَحْزَنَ وَالِدَيْهِ فَقَدْ عَقَّهُمَا.

The Commander of the Faithful (peace be upon him) has said: "One who causes his parents to become sad has indeed been disowned by them."

Bihārul Anwār, Volume 74, Page 64

## Ḥadīth Number 30
## The Imam's Displeasure

عن أَبي جَعْفَرٍ عليه السلام قَالَ: إِنَّ أَبي نَظَرَ إِلَى رَجُلٍ وَ مَعَهُ ابْنُهُ يَمْشي وَ الإِبْنُ مُتَّكِئٌ عَلَى ذِرَاعِ الأَبِ قَالَ فَمَا كَلَّمَهُ أَبي عليه السلام مَقْتاً لَهُ حَتَّى فَارَقَ الدُّنْيَا.

Imām Muḥammad al-Bāqir (peace be upon him) relates: "Once my father saw a person and his son walking together. As they walked, the son was leaning against the arm of his father. (This act of the son was so abhorrent and infuriating to my father that) he (peace be upon him) never spoke to him throughout his life."

Biḥārul Anwār, Volume 74, Page 64

## Ḥadīth Number 31
## Quarrelling with One's Father

قَالَ أَبُو عَبْدِ اللَّهِ ﷺ: ثَلاَثَةٌ مَنْ عَازَهُمْ ذَلَّ الْوَالِدُ وَ السُّلْطَانُ وَ الْغَرِيــمُ.

Imām as-Ṣādiq (peace be upon him) said: "There are three individuals that whoever argues with them shall suffer humiliation and disgrace: one's father; a (just) ruler; and one in debt."

Biḥārul Anwār, Volume 74, Page 71

## Ḥadīth Number 32
## Fragrance Of Paradise

قَالَ رَسُولُ اللّٰهِ ﷺ فِي كَلَامٍ لَهُ: إِيَّاكُمْ وَ عُقُوقَ الْوَالِدَيْنِ فَإِنَّ رِيحَ الْجَنَّةِ تُوجَدُ مِنْ مَسِيرَةِ أَلْفِ عَامٍ وَ لاَ يَجِدُهَا عَاقٌّ وَ لاَ قَاطِعُ رَحِمٍ.

The Messenger of Allāh (peace be upon him and his family) has said: "Beware of become disowned by your parents, for verily the fragrance of paradise which can be smelt from a distance of a thousand years, shall never reach the nostrils of one who has been disowned by his parents and one who has severed the bonds of kinship (with his relatives)."

Biḥārul Anwār, Volume 74, Page 62

## Ḥadīth Number 33
## No Entry Into Paradise!

عَنِ الصَّادِقِ ﷺ قَالَ: لاَ يَدْخُلُ الْجَنَّةَ الْعَاقُ لِوَالِدَيهِ وَ الْمُدْمِنُ الْخَمْرِ وَ الْمَنَّانُ بِأَفْعَالِ الْخَيْرِ إِذَا عَمِلَهُ.

Imām as-Ṣādiq (peace be upon him) has said: "The person who has been disowned by his parents, one who consumes intoxicants and one who does acts of goodness towards others but imposes obligations upon them shall never enter into Paradise."

Biḥārul Anwār, Volume 74, Page 74

## Ḥadīth Number 34
## Allāh Shall Not Exhibit Mercy Upon Them!

قَالَ رَسُولُ اللّهِ ﷺ: أَرْبَعَةٌ لاَ يَنْظُرُ اللّهُ إِلَيْهِمْ يَوْمَ الْقِيَامَةِ عَاقٌّ وَ مَنَّانٌ وَ مُكَذِّبٌ بِالْقَدَرِ وَ مُدْمِنُ خَمْرٍ.

The Messenger of Allāh (peace be upon him and his family) has stated: "On the Day of Judgment there shall be four groups of people upon whom Allāh shall not cast His look of mercy: those who have been disowned by their parents, those who place obligations upon others after doing good to them, those who reject the concept of fate and destiny and the one who consumes intoxicants."

Biḥārul Anwār, Volume 74, Page 71

## Ḥadīth Number 35
## Chastisement In This World

قَالَ رَسُولُ اللّهِ ﷺ: ثَلاَثَةٌ مِنَ الذُّنُوبِ تُعَجَّلُ عُقُوبَتُهَا وَ لاَ تُؤَخَّرُ إِلَى الأَخِرَةِ عُقُوقُ الْوَالِدَيْنِ وَ الْبَغْيُ عَلَى النَّاسِ وَ كُفْرُ الإِحْسَانِ.

The Messenger of Allāh (peace be upon him and his family) has stated: "There are three sins, the punishments of which are hastened and not deferred for the hereafter: disownment by one's parents, committing oppression upon the people, and ingratitude with respect to kindness."

Biḥārul Anwār, Volume 74, Page 74

## Hadīth Number 36
## The Grave Sin

عَنْ أَبِي عَبْدِ اللهِ ﷺ قَالَ: أَلذُّنُوبُ الَّتِي تَظْلُمُ الْهَوَاءَ عُقُوقُ الْوَالِدَينِ.

Imām as-Ṣādiq (peace be upon him) has said: "A sin that darkens the skies is being disowned by one's parents."

Biḥārul Anwār, Volume 74, Page 74

## Ḥadīth Number 37
## Wretchedness

عَنِ الصَّادِقِ ﷺ قَالَ: عُقُوقُ الْوَالِدَيْنِ مِنَ الْكَبَائِرِ لِأَنَّ اللَّهَ جَعَلَ الْعَاقَّ عَصِيّاً شَقِيّاً.

Imām aṣ-Ṣādiq (peace be upon him) has stated: "Becoming disowned by one's parents is one of the Great Sins. This is because Allāh, the Mighty and the Glorious, has termed such a person disobedient and wretched."

Biḥārul Anwār, Volume 74, Page 74

# Ḥadīth Number 38
## Perdition

عَنْ أَبِي عَبْدِ اللهِ ﷺ أَنَّ رَسُولَ اللهِ ﷺ حَضَرَ شَابّاً عِنْدَ وَفَاتِهِ فَقَالَ: لَهُ قُلْ لَا إِلَهَ إِلَّا اللَّهُ. قَالَ: فَاعْتُقِلَ لِسَانُهُ مِرَاراً. فَقَالَ لِامْرَأَةٍ عِنْدَ رَأْسِهِ: هَلْ لِهَذَا أُمٌّ؟ قَالَتْ: نَعَمْ أَنَا أُمُّهُ. قَالَ: أَفَسَاخِطَةٌ [أَنْتِ] عَلَيْهِ؟ قَالَتْ: نَعَمْ مَا كَلَّمْتُهُ مُنْذُ سِتِّ حِجَجٍ. قَالَ لَهَا: ارْضَيْ عَنْهُ. قَالَتْ: رَضِيَ اللَّهُ عَنْهُ بِرِضَاكَ عَنْهُ يَا رَسُولَ اللهِ. فَقَالَ لَهُ رَسُولُ اللهِ ﷺ: قُلْ لَا إِلَهَ إِلَّا اللَّهُ. قَالَ فَقَالَهَا. ثُمَّ طَفَا.

Imām as-Ṣādiq (peace be upon him) relates: "Once, the Messenger of Allāh (peace be upon him and his family) approached a youth who was on the verge of dying, and said to him: "Say 'There is no God except Allāh.' But the youth's tongue appeared to be tied and he was unable utter the words. When this took place several times, the Prophet said to a lady standing near the youth's head: "Does this youth have a mother?" The lady replied: "Yes, I am his mother." The Prophet asked her: "Are you angry with him?" She confessed: "Yes. I have not spoken to him for the last six years." Hearing this, he said to her: "Be pleased with him." She agreed and said: "O' Prophet of Allāh! For the sake of your pleasure, may Allāh be pleased with him." (Then, turning to the youth) he said: "Say 'There is no God, except Allāh')." (This time) the youth was able to recite the words and shortly afterwards, his soul departed his body."

Biḥārul Anwār, Volume 74, Page 75

## Ḥadīth Number 39
## Acts Without Benefits

قَالَ رَسُولُ اللَّهُ ﷺ: يُقَالُ لِلْعَاقِّ إِعْمَلْ مَا شِئْتَ فَإِنِّي لاَ أَغْفِرُ لَكَ وَ يُقَالُ لِلْبَارِّ إِعْمَلْ مَا شِئْتَ فَإِنِّي سَأَغْفِرُ لَكَ.

The Messenger of Allāh (peace be upon him and his family) has said: "One who has been disowned by his parents is told: 'Act as you please, for I shall not forgive you.' Whereas one who is good towards his parents is told, 'Act as you please. I will be forgiving towards you.'"

Biḥārul Anwār, Volume 74, Page 80